Extraordinary Lives

NAPOLEON BONAPARTE

Judith Anderson

WAYLAND

First published in 2010 by Wayland

Copyright © Wayland 2010

Wayland
338 Euston Road
London NW1 3BH

Wayland Australia
Level 17/207 Kent Street
Sydney NSW 2000

Editor: Katie Powell
Designer: Phipps Design
Picture Researcher: Shelley Noronha

British Library Cataloguing in Publication Data

Anderson, Judith.
    Napoleon. – (Extraordinary lives)
    1. Napoleon I, Emperor of the French, 1769-1821–Juvenile literature.
    2. Emperors–France–Biography–Juvenile literature.
    3. France–History–Consulate and First Empire, 1799-1815–Juvenile literature.
    I. Title II. Series
    944'.05'092-dc22

ISBN: 978 0 7502 6052 7

Picture acknowledgements: Cover © Getty Images, p4 © Napoleon (1769-1821) Giving Orders before the Battle of Austerlitz, 2nd December 1805, 1808 by Vernet, Antoine Charles Horace (Carle) (1758-1836) Chateau de Versailles, France / Lauros / Giraudon/ The Bridgeman Art Library, p5 © Getty Images, p6 © Wayland Picture Library, p7 © The Art Archive / Napoleonic Museum Rome / Gianni Dagli Ortil,p8 © The Art Archive / Bibliothèque des Arts Décoratifs Paris / Gianni Dagli Orti, p9 © RA/Lebrecht Music & Arts, p10 © The Art Archive / Musée Carnavalet Paris / Gianni Dagli Orti, p11 © The Art Archive / Musée Carnavalet Paris / Gianni Dagli Orti, p12 © Wayland Picture Library (NPG), p13 © The Art Archive / Malmaison Musée du Chateau / Gianni Dagli Orti, p14 © Battle of Pyramids, 21 July 1798 by Watteau, Francois Louis Joseph (1758-1823) Musee des Beaux-Arts, Valenciennes, France / Lauros / Giraudon / The Bridgeman Art Library, p15 © RA/Lebrecht Music & Arts, p16 © The Art Archive / Musée du Château de Versailles / Alfredo Dagli Orti, p17 © The Art Archive / Kharbine-Tapabor, p18 © Wayland Picture Library, p19 © The Art Archive/ Musée du Château de Versailles / Gianni Dagli Orti, p20 © Wayland Picture Library, p21 © The Entry of the French into Moscow, 14 September 1812, engraved by Edme Bovinet (1767- 1832) (aquatint) by Couche, Louis Francois (1782-1849) (after) Private Collection / The Stapleton Collection / The Bridgeman Art Library, p22 © 'Cossack Sports or the Platoff Hunt in Full Cry after French Game' by William Elmes, 1813 Private Collection / The Bridgeman Art Library, p23 © The Art Archive / Musée de L'Armée Paris / Gianni Dagli Orti, p24 © The Art Archive / Musée de L'Armée Paris / Gianni Dagli Orti, p25 © The Death of Napoleon Bonaparte (1769-1821) c.1840 by French School, (19th century) Bibliotheque Nationale, Paris, France / Archives Charmet / The Bridgeman Art Library, p26 ©AFP / Getty Images, p27 © iStock

Every effort has been made to clear copyright. Should there be any inadvertent omission, please apply to the publisher for rectification.

Printed in China

Wayland is a division of Hachette Children's Books, an Hachette UK company.
www.hachette.co.uk

Contents

Words that appear in **bold** can be
found in the glossary.

Napoleon Bonaparte – an extraordinary emperor

On a cold day at Austerlitz in December 1805, Napoleon Bonaparte, Emperor of France, woke early and stepped out of his tent. It was difficult to see through the thick fog that swirled about him, but Napoleon knew his enemies were waiting.

Enemies

Napoleon's enemies were the Emperors of Russia and Austria. Their combined armies were much bigger than the French army and Napoleon's men were far from home. But Napoleon had been planning this battle for weeks. Now, by hiding some of his troops, he had tricked his enemies into thinking that the French army was weak. As dawn broke, the Russians gave the order to attack.

Napoleon, on his white horse Marengo, gives orders to his generals at the Battle of Austerlitz.

The Battle of Austerlitz

The battle was fierce. The **infantry** fought with rifles and **bayonets**. Soldiers on horseback cut their way through with swords while the **artillery** bombarded the battlefield with cannon fire. Then, Napoleon gave the order for his hidden troops to attack. The Russian and Austrian armies were horrified to see a new wave of French soldiers advancing out of the mist.

Jacques Louis David's portrait of Napoleon shows the emperor in his most famous pose.

Soldiers flee

By late afternoon, France's enemies were fleeing across some frozen ponds. Napoleon ordered his artillery to fire into the ponds to break up the ice. Many soldiers drowned in their icy depths.

The Battle of Austerlitz was Napoleon's greatest victory. He'd won new lands for France and proved that his army was the best in Europe. Yet Napoleon wasn't from a royal family; he hadn't even been born in France. So, how had he risen to such glory?

NAPOLEON'S IMAGE

Napoleon is often remembered as a short man who wore his hat sideways and tucked his right hand inside his waistcoat. The truth is, his height was average and he may have worn his hat sideways because this was how ordinary soldiers wore theirs. However, the hand in his waistcoat was probably a fashion statement – lots of officers stood like that in the eighteenth century!

A Corsican childhood

Napoleon Bonaparte was born in 1769, on a small island called Corsica in the Mediterranean Sea. The Bonapartes were one of the most important families on the island. Napoleon's father, Carlo, was a lawyer. His mother, Letizia, married Carlo when she was only 14 years old. Napoleon was the second of eight children.

Family life

Napoleon wasn't very close to his family. He disliked his father, while his mother was strict and thought nothing of beating her children with a stick if they were disobedient.

Carlo and Letizia had big plans for Napoleon and his brother Joseph. In December 1778, the boys were sent to school in France. Nine-year-old Napoleon went to the military school at Brienne. This was an unusual thing for a Corsican boy to do and despite his determination to succeed as a soldier, he missed the warm sunshine and the countryside around his home.

This maps shows what Europe was like in the late eighteenth century.

FAMILY CONNECTIONS

Family background was very important in the eighteenth century. If you wanted to get a good job in the military you had to belong to a **noble** family or have powerful friends close to the French King Louis XVI in Paris.

However, many Corsican families, such as the Bonapartes, were actually descended from Italian families and Corsica had only recently become part of France. No one had heard of the Bonapartes in Paris, so Carlo and Letizia sought help from the governor of Corsica to get Napoleon into the military school at Brienne. They thought this would be his best chance to get ahead.

Letizia Bonaparte was a strict mother, both feared and respected by Napoleon. He later gave her the title 'Madame Mere'.

A military education

Napoleon felt isolated at Brienne. Other boys made fun of his Corsican accent and his loyalty to his island home, while his teachers weren't particularly interested in a sullen boy with no military background. Yet he was stubborn and tough, and showed a particular flair for mathematics, science and history.

Schoolday antics

One of the most famous stories about Napoleon's schooldays concerns a snowball fight in the grounds at Brienne. After a heavy fall of snow, Napoleon suggested that the boys build a fortress. He then directed a battle between the **besiegers** and the **besieged**. The fight ended when some boys placed rocks inside their snowballs, but the incident shows Napoleon's growing interest in military strategy.

This is the impressive Ecole Militaire in Paris. Napoleon had few friends there, but studied hard.

Ecole Militaire

Napoleon had hoped to join the **navy** when he left Brienne, but the navy wasn't interested in a boy from Corsica. So, in 1784, at the age of 15, he took a place as a **cadet** at the famous Ecole Militaire in Paris. At that time, the French capital was a city of huge contrasts; the wealth of a few and the **poverty** of many. The extravagance of Napoleon's fellow cadets shocked him deeply.

After much hard work he took his exams a year early, showing an exceptional ability in mathematics that helped him win a place in an elite artillery **regiment**. In September 1785, just a month after his sixteenth birthday, Napoleon became an officer of the French army.

This is how a typical young French officer in the 1790s, such as Napoleon, would have dressed.

ITALIAN ROOTS

One of the most extraordinary facts about Napoleon was that he did not speak French until the age of nine. Although he grew up to be Emperor of France, he and his family spoke Italian at home in Corsica. Indeed, Napoleon's name was spelled the Italian way, *Napoleone Buonaparte*, until he changed it to make it sound more French.

The young officer

Napoleon was an ambitious young officer. He wanted to fight France's foreign enemies but the French people had overthrown King Louis XVI by 1793 and had set up a **revolutionary government**. Napoleon's job was to help maintain order within France's borders.

Promotion

Napoleon's military skills were first noticed at Toulon in 1793, when he pretended to attack some **anti-revolutionary** forces from one side while planning an attack on the other side. His plan succeeded and he was promoted to **brigadier-general**.

However Paris was full of rumours, and some people suspected Napoleon was not loyal to the government. Then, in 1795, the chance came to prove himself. When he heard of a plan to attack the government, he used cannon fire to repel the enemy. For this he was promoted to **general**.

This is a portrait of King Louis XVI in all his royal finery, before the monarchy was overthrown.

REVOLUTION!

The French Revolution began in 1789. People were angry about the power of the bishops and nobles and the extravagance of the royal family. They hated the high **taxes** and the high price of bread. **Riots** on the streets led to a revolutionary government that tried to make laws and taxes fairer. These were violent times. The king was beheaded in 1793 and many nobles had to flee the country while mass executions swept through France.

Napoleon hated the riots and the executions. Yet he supported the revolutionary government because he, too, hated the power of the French king and his 'favourites'. He wanted a strong government, and the revolution meant that he, an insignificant Corsican, would no longer be looked down upon. The revolution turned Napoleon into a Frenchman.

Revolutionaries can be seen here storming the Tuileries Palace in Paris, 10 August 1792.

Victory in Italy

As a reward for his success in Paris in 1795, Napoleon was given command of the French Army of Italy. This army's role was to defeat France's enemies in Italy and push the Austrians back over the Alps. Napoleon had longed to fight on foreign soil and he was determined to lead his men to victory.

Napoleon conquers

By early 1797, Napoleon's army had conquered most of northern Italy. One of his most successful tactics was to use his soldiers to drive a wedge through the opposing side and defeat each half separately. He often used cannons and always pursued a fleeing army. However, Napoleon wasn't just a great planner; he also took risks and sometimes fought directly alongside his men.

A soldier's life

At the start of the campaign, the French Army of Italy was underfed and underpaid. Napoleon knew he needed to keep his men happy so he allowed them to **plunder** towns and villages to provide them with food and clothing and also to reward them.

This painting shows Napoleon leading a charge across the bridge at Arcole, Italy in 1796.

Napoleon was popular with his men and often handed out gifts and honours. Yet discipline was very important to Napoleon. Soldiers soon feared and admired him in equal measure.

After 18 months of fighting, the Austrians had been chased out of Italy. No one was in any doubt that Napoleon was the victor. The French government was thrilled with all the **looted** treasure he had sent them. Now, Napoleon could return to Paris to be with his new wife, Josephine.

Napoleon adored his wife Josephine and wrote her passionate letters from Italy. She, however, was more interested in his fame and money!

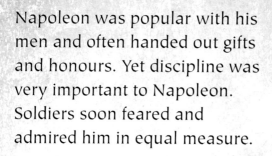

HYGIENE!

Napoleon spent many years travelling huge distances in hostile environments. Yet he hated the cold and insisted on taking a scalding hot bath every day. Hygiene was important to him and he cleaned his teeth regularly with a silver-handled brush, unlike his wife, Josephine whose teeth were black and rotten!

The Egyptian campaign

The Austrians weren't the only enemies of France. Most of Europe was hostile, and Britain, just a few miles across the English Channel, was the biggest enemy of them all. However, Napoleon knew that **invading** Britain would be difficult because the British navy was more powerful than the French navy. Napoleon began to look for other ways to harm Britain.

The East

One way was to go to Egypt and cut off the vital British **trade route** to India. The French government was happy to send Napoleon to Egypt. His success in Italy had made him very popular and they were worried that if he stayed in Paris he might become too powerful.

At the Battle of the Pyramids in 1798, Napoleon formed his battalions into squares to repel the Mamluks' cavalry charges.

This suited Napoleon, who was fascinated by the East and had big plans for the area. As well as his army he took scientists and artists with him to investigate Egypt's riches and record their findings.

However, conquering Egypt wasn't easy. The Egyptian soldiers (known as Mamluks) were great warriors and the French army also had to fight **dehydration** and disease in the desert heat. Then, in 1798, a decisive battle was fought near the pyramids and the Mamluks were defeated by Napoleon's battalions, which he formed into squares. Napoleon admired the Mamluks' bravery but afterwards he was brutal towards any Egyptians who opposed him.

Thousands of Mamluks died at the Battle of the Pyramids, while Napoleon reported that only 29 Frenchmen lost their lives.

The British attack

A few weeks after the battle, Napoleon received some disastrous news. The British, led by Admiral Nelson, had sunk the **fleet** of French ships at Aboukir Bay and the French army was now stranded. Meanwhile, Napoleon's spies reported that the French armies were losing elsewhere in Europe. So, in 1799, he decided to return to Paris in secret to avoid capture by Nelson.

First Consul

When Napoleon returned to Paris in 1779, France was in a mess. The government had no money, the Austrians and the Russians were threatening to invade and some people even wanted to bring back the royal family.

A powerful man

Some officials thought Napoleon would make an excellent ruler, so they plotted with him to get rid of the old government and, in 1799, they appointed him **First Consul**, the most powerful man in France. Napoleon's bullying tactics weren't always liked, but people were pleased when he brought order to Paris and won more battles.

First were the Austrians, who had regained lands taken by Napoleon during his first Italian campaign. Napoleon knew that no one would expect him to lead an army with its heavy cannons over the Alps, so this is exactly what he did! He triumphed at the Battle of Marengo but, by now, his army was exhausted. Europe was fed up with fighting. It was time to make peace.

This painting shows Napoleon crossing the Alps on his favourite horse, Marengo. In fact he made the journey on a donkey, but he knew this wouldn't look quite so impressive!

FRANCE AND BRITAIN

When Napoleon became First Consul, one of his greatest ambitions was to invade Britain. The two countries were bitter enemies and Britain had been a friend to Austria – France's other **foe**. Napoleon wanted a French empire with French influence around the world and the only way he could achieve this was by crushing his rival across the English Channel.

So, when Napoleon made peace with both Austria and Britain at the end of 1801, he knew it wasn't permanent. A few years of peace would give him enough time to recover and build up a superior invasion force. Napoleon hadn't finished with all the fighting. Not by a long way!

This artist's impression from 1803 shows ideas for an invasion tunnel under the English Channel.

Order and power

Napoleon stayed in France for the next two years (1801–03) and began to make important changes to the way the country was run. He wasn't really interested in the rights of poor people, but he knew that a steady supply of money, a good transport system and new laws would help him stay in power.

Roads and rewards

Napoleon set up the Bank of France to control the supply of money. He ordered the building of new roads, canals and bridges to make travelling faster and easier. He also brought in new laws to make the government and legal system more efficient. Some of these laws became known as the **Napoleonic Code**. They weren't always fairer than the old laws, but they were simpler and easier to enforce.

After Napoleon's coronation he awarded many lands and titles to his brothers and sisters.

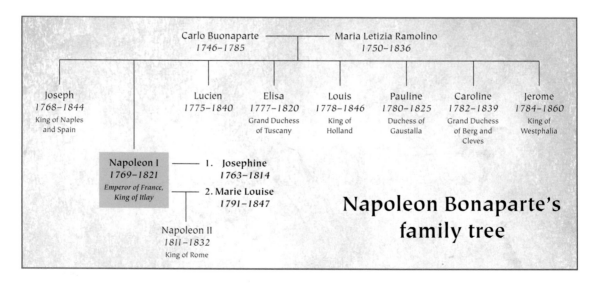

Carlo Buonaparte 1746–1785 — Maria Letizia Ramolino 1750–1836

Joseph 1768–1844 King of Naples and Spain

Lucien 1775–1840

Elisa 1777–1820 Grand Duchess of Tuscany

Louis 1778–1846 King of Holland

Pauline 1780–1825 Duchess of Gaustalla

Caroline 1782–1839 Grand Duchess of Berg and Cleves

Jerome 1784–1860 King of Westphalia

Napoleon I 1769–1821 Emperor of France, King of Itlay

1. Josephine 1763–1814
2. Marie Louise 1791–1847

Napoleon II 1811–1832 King of Rome

Napoleon Bonaparte's family tree

Some people thought Napoleon wanted too much power for himself. Many attempts were made to kidnap or **assassinate** him. But Napoleon had lots of spies and always punished the plotters. He also rewarded his favourites. A new reward called *The Legion of Honour* kept his loyal supporters happy.

Emperor of France

Then, in 1804, a vote was held and Napoleon became Emperor of France. This meant that he and his descendants could rule France forever. His coronation was just like the coronations of the old kings of France, except for one important difference. No one else was allowed to place the crown on his head. Napoleon did it himself!

As Emperor, Napoleon decided to give his relatives some of the lands he had conquered in Europe. He didn't always get on with his family and none of them liked his wife, Josephine, so he hoped that this would stop them meddling in his affairs. It wasn't easy, re-organising France and ruling Italy while dealing with family squabbles!

Napoleon wanted to look powerful. Compare this picture of him wearing his coronation robes with the portrait of King Louis XVI on page 10.

Return to war

In the summer of 1803, war between France and Britain broke out again. For two years, Napoleon had been preparing his troops along the coast of France, ready for a cross-Channel invasion. But, of course, Napoleon was a soldier, not a sailor.

A British invasion

Things did not go well for Napoleon this time. As a soldier, he didn't understand the treacherous tides. Either the weather was against him, his plans were too complicated, or his admiral, Villeneuve, refused to follow his orders. Eventually, on 21 October 1805, the French fleet was destroyed by the British navy under Admiral Nelson at the Battle of Trafalgar.

This map shows the extent of Napoleon's influence in Europe at the height of the French empire in 1811.

Europe 1811

Key
France
Areas of French occupation or influence

DENMARK

GRAND DUCHY OF WARSAW

UNITED KINGDOM

PRUSSIA

GERMAN STATES

RUSSIA

AUSTRIA

FRANCE

ITALY

PORTUGAL

SPAIN

CORSICA

Mediterranean Sea

By this time however, Austria and Russia were attacking French territory in the east, so Napoleon led his army back across Europe. All that training along the coast was put to good use. No one expected the army to march 20 miles a day, but they were fit and well-fed. Then, Napoleon won the Battle of Austerlitz (see pages 4–5). On land, at least, he seemed invincible.

This artist's impression shows Napoleon's Grand Army marching through Russia towards Moscow.

Napoleon's Grand Army

Stories about Napoleon and his 'Grand Army' began to appear in newspapers across Europe. Nursery rhymes and cartoons exaggerated tales of the 'Corsican Ogre' who caused havoc on the battlefield. Some people even believed that Napoleon could fly!

By 1807, Napoleon had forced Russia and Prussia to sign peace **treaties** that gave him control of territories in Poland and the German states. He couldn't fly, but Napoleon was now the most powerful man in Europe.

SUPERSTITIONS

For such a clever man, Napoleon was remarkably superstitious. He believed he had a 'lucky star' that watched over him. He also had a fear of open doors and thought Fridays brought bad luck.

The road to retreat

By 1810, the French empire had gained vast new territories. But Napoleon was worried that he didn't have an **heir** to **succeed** him. He divorced Josephine and married Marie Louise, the daughter of his old enemy, the Austrian Emperor, in the hope that she would give him a son.

More troubles for Napoleon

There were other problems, too. Spain had joined the war against France and this meant Napoleon was fighting in several different countries at once. Despite Napoleon's successes, many French soldiers died or were wounded. With the British navy blocking French **ports**, **supplies** were running out.

March to Russia

Yet Napoleon wasn't ready to stop fighting. He decided to push east to conquer Russia. After all, his Grand Army could march anywhere – couldn't it?

Napoleon captured Moscow in September 1812, but the Russians set fire to the city to stop French looting. Although the French army were victorious, the soldiers had nothing to eat and Napoleon was forced to retreat.

This British cartoon shows Napoleon as a fox fleeing from the Russians.

FEEDING AN ARMY

The **Napoleonic wars** lasted from 1803 to 1814. Napoleon was constantly travelling and he understood the difficulty of feeding his huge army on the move. He famously declared that 'an army marches on its stomach', and offered 12,000 **francs** to anyone who could invent a way to stop fresh food going off. Eventually, a French man called Nicolas Appert discovered a way to **preserve** food by sealing it in a glass jar and boiling it. When Napoleon tasted his bottled meat and gravy, Appert won the prize money. However, even bottled meat had to be transported somehow. Moscow was just that little bit too far for soldiers to carry the food supplies they needed.

The freezing Russian winter killed many French soldiers as they retreated from Moscow.

Defeat and exile

By 1813, the Prussian and Austrian armies could see that France was weak and they began to attack across her borders along with Spain and Britain. Napoleon led his men into battle once more but it was too late and, in March 1814, Paris was captured.

This portrait of Napoleon abdicating in 1814 shows him as a brooding, angry man.

An isolated emperor

On 6 April 1814, Emperor Napoleon was forced to give up his titles and power. The other rulers of Europe brought back the royal family and crowned Louis XVII as the King of France. This was a bitter blow for Napoleon, who was sent to live on the island of Elba, off the coast of Italy.

Napoleon's return

Napoleon couldn't accept that France didn't need him so, after a few months on Elba, he plotted his return. With the help of some loyal officers, he sailed to France and journeyed to Paris, gathering a small army along the way. When Louis XVII heard who was coming he fled and Napoleon once again ruled France for a brief period known as 'The Hundred Days'.

The Battle of Waterloo

But Napoleon's old enemies had got rid of him once and would do so again. The British and the Prussian armies defeated the French at the Battle of Waterloo in 1815. This time Napoleon was banished to an island from which he would never escape: St. Helena, in the middle of the Pacific Ocean.

Napoleon remained on St. Helena until his death in 1821. He never saw France, or his wife and son (also called Napoleon) again. Instead he wrote his memoirs – lengthy accounts of his campaigns, his strategies and his victories. He exaggerated his successes and downplayed his failings. More than anything, Napoleon wanted to be remembered as a brilliant soldier and leader.

POISONED?

Napoleon probably died of stomach cancer, but some people think he was poisoned with **arsenic**. Certainly, traces of arsenic have been found in his remains, though this may have been absorbed from the green paint used on the walls of the house where he lived on St. Helena.

This is an artist's impression of Napoleon's deathbed scene at Longwood House, St. Helena.

Why is Napoleon Bonaparte important today?

Napoleon is one of the most written about figures in history. His name is recognised throughout the world and he has been portrayed in many films, cartoons and documentaries. Part of the reason for this fame is due to his own determination to be remembered.

Triumphs and failures

During his lifetime, Napoleon **commissioned** many portraits of himself. He always tried to look impressive, and most painters were happy to show him in his best light. The same is true of his memoirs. His readers soon forgot the disasters and the mistakes and remembered him for his triumphs.

The *Legion of Honour* that Napoleon founded is still used today. Here, French President Nicolas Sarkozy awards the medal to British sailor Ellen MacArthur.

For Napoleon *was* a great soldier and leader. He changed the way armies were recruited, trained and rewarded, and his ruthless battle tactics brought a new kind of **warfare** to Europe. He experimented with square battle formations, lightweight artillery, Appert's food preservation system and many other ideas that were eventually copied by his enemies.

A modern man

Napoleon was also a moderniser away from the battlefield. Many of the roads, bridges, schools and universities he established in France are still in use today. He supported the study of science and his Napoleonic Code became the foundation for other legal systems around the world.

Religious views

Napoleon's influence remains in other, less obvious ways, too. Many French revolutionaries wanted to get rid of religion, but Napoleon was more tolerant. He allowed **Catholicism** to remain as the official religion of France and he tried to stop people **persecuting Jews**.

But perhaps his greatest influence is seen in the way Europe views itself. Some people think the origins of the **European Union** can be found in Napoleon's vision of a Europe united under his rule. Certainly, countries learned to make **alliances** with each other. In the end, their unity was the only way to defeat Napoleon.

The Arc de Triomphe in Paris was commissioned by Napoleon in 1806 after his victory at Austerlitz.

A walk through the life of Napoleon Bonaparte

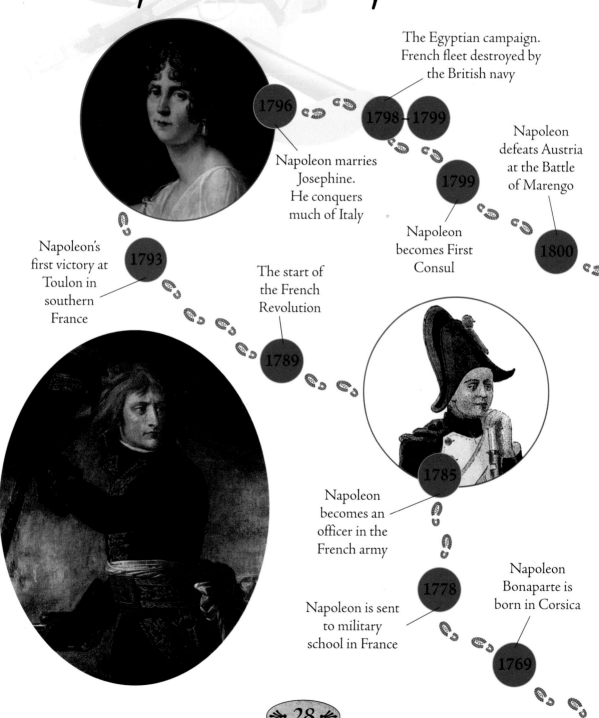

1796
Napoleon marries Josephine. He conquers much of Italy

The Egyptian campaign. French fleet destroyed by the British navy
1798–1799

Napoleon defeats Austria at the Battle of Marengo

1799
Napoleon becomes First Consul

1800

Napoleon's first victory at Toulon in southern France
1793

The start of the French Revolution
1789

1785
Napoleon becomes an officer in the French army

Napoleon is sent to military school in France
1778

Napoleon Bonaparte is born in Corsica
1769

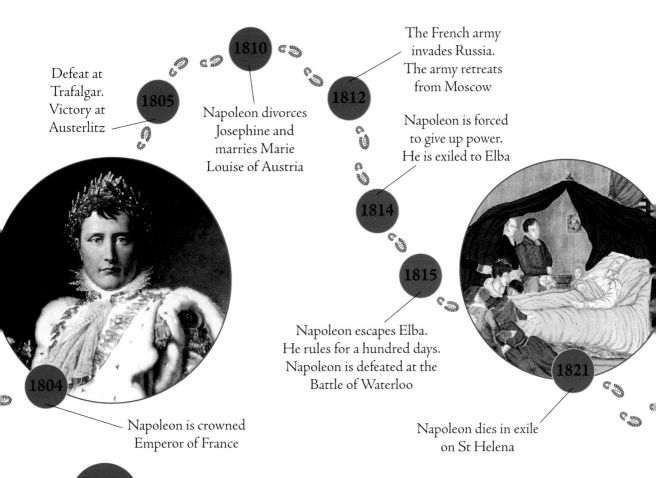

1810

Defeat at Trafalgar. Victory at Austerlitz

1805

Napoleon divorces Josephine and marries Marie Louise of Austria

The French army invades Russia. The army retreats from Moscow

1812

Napoleon is forced to give up power. He is exiled to Elba

1814

1815

1804

Napoleon is crowned Emperor of France

Napoleon escapes Elba. He rules for a hundred days. Napoleon is defeated at the Battle of Waterloo

1821

Napoleon dies in exile on St Helena

Cross-curricular links

Use this topic web to explore the life of Napoleon Bonaparte in different areas of your curriculum.

MATHEMATICS

The metric system was introduced in France during the Revolution. Britain refused to use the metric system and still uses the old imperial measurement of miles. Why do you think Britain chose not to use it?

ART

The painting of Napoleon on page 16 shows Napoleon on his horse. He actually rode a donkey over the Alps. What message does this portrait say about him?

NAPOLEON BONAPARTE

GEOGRAPHY

Napoleon's Grand Army marched through many different countries. What sorts of climates would these men have encountered on their travels in Russia, Spain and Egypt?

LANGUAGE

Lots of English words come from France. Many are to do with food, fashion and culture such as 'cafe' and 'theatre'. These were things that Britain most admired about France during Napoleon's time. Can you think of any other words?

SCIENCE

Napoleon encouraged scientists by establishing scientific institutes and offering prizes for new discoveries, such as Appert's food preservation system. Can you find out about any other discoveries?

Glossary

alliances Agreements promising mutual support.

anti-revolutionary Against revolution; supporting the king.

arsenic A type of poison.

artillery Big guns, such as cannons.

assassinate The murder of a leader.

battalions Units of soldiers. Each batallion had its own commander.

bayonets Sharp knives attached to the ends of rifles.

besieged To be attacked within a stronghold.

besiegers The attackers of a stronghold.

brigadier-general A rank of officer in the army.

cadet someone training to be an officer in the army.

Catholicism A Christian faith with the Pope as its spiritual leader.

cavalry Soldiers who fought on horseback.

commissioned An order for something to be produced.

dehydration A severe lack of water.

European Union A group of European countries united by mutual agreement.

First Consul A powerful role in France.

fleet A large group of ships.

foe An enemy.

francs The old currency of France.

general A high rank of officer in the army.

heir Someone who will take over a title after their parent dies.

infantry Foot soldiers.

invading To send troops to take over another country.

Jews People of the Jewish faith.

looted Stolen.

Napoleonic Code A series of laws developed under Napoleon.

Napoleonic wars A series of conflicts fought between France and other European countries.

navy The ships and sailors that defend a country.

noble To be born into aristocratic or high-ranking families.

persecuting Singling out for punishment.

plunder Steal.

ports Coastal towns with harbours.

poverty Living in very poor conditions.

preserve To keep for a long time.

regiment A military unit.

revolutionaries People who use force to try to overthrow a government.

revolutionary government A government that overthrows the previous ruler to bring about change.

riots Violent protests.

succeed To rule after someone.

supplies All the food, clothing, weapons and equipment an army needs.

taxes Money that people have to pay to their ruler or government.

trade route The route taken by goods travelling from one country to another.

treaties Formal agreements between two or more countries.

warfare To be involved in a war.

Index

Numbers in **bold** refer to photographs or illustrations.

Further Information

More books to read

Extraordinary Lives: Horatio Nelson by Jane Bingham (Wayland, 2010)

My Napoleon by Catherine Brighton (Frances Lincoln, 1998)

Questioning History: The French Revolution by Nicola Barber (Wayland, 2008)

Who Was Napoleon: The Little General Who Wanted to Rule the World by Adrian Hadland (Short Books, 2005)

Places to visit

- National Army Museum, London
- Arc de Triomphe, Paris
- Ecole Militaire, Paris

Useful websites

www.kidspast.com/world-history/0390-napoleons-empire.php
This website offers an overview of Napoleon's life and achievements.

www.channel4.com/history/microsites/H/history/napoleon/leaders1.html
A biography of Napoleon.

www.bbc.co.uk/history/historic_figures/bonaparte-napoleon.shtm
The BBC website has lots of facts about Napoleon and the French Revolution.

Extraordinary Lives

Contents of titles in the series:

WAYLAND